Boom Boom Classics!

For Boomwhackers® Musical Tubes

- **10 Classic Themes by Great Composers**
- **Cool CD With Full Performance and Accompaniment Tracks**
- **Teaching Suggestions and Reproducible Visuals**
- **Kid-Tested!**

This is a joint publication between Warner Bros. Publications and Whacky Music, Inc.

BOOMWHACKERS® Tuned Percussion Tubes are a product of Whacky Music, Inc., of Sedona, Arizona.

"BOOMWHACKERS" is a registered trademark licensed to Whacky Music, Inc. Visit the Whacky Music Web site at www.boomwhackers.com.

Special thanks to our wonderful field-testers,
the sixth-grade music classes from Good Shepherd Episcopal School in Dallas, Texas, and
their teacher/director, Chris Judah-Lauder

Arranger/Consultant: Chris Judah-Lauder
Managing Editor: James Grupenhoff
Consulting Editor: Gayle Giese
Recording Producer: Teena Chinn
Cover Design: Candy Woolley
Music Engraving: Mark Burgess
Text Layout: Lauren Hughes
Text Editor: Nadine DeMarco
Production Coordinator: Sheryl Rose

M000121930

General Teaching Suggestions

Although teaching suggestions are provided for each song, here are some general tips to help you and your students thoroughly enjoy playing the nine fall and winter holiday songs in this collection.

Use the cool CD that is included! The Boomwhacker® parts were recorded live in the studio and were not sampled or synthesized. Before teaching the Boomwhacker® parts for a particular song, play the full performance version on the CD so that students will get the song in their ears. After students are familiar with the song, assign parts and distribute the Boomwhackers®.

Reproducible teaching visuals are provided for most songs. These visuals may be photocopied as handouts for the students or used as transparencies.

Once students have the skills to play through the entire song, they will enjoy playing and performing with the accompaniment tracks on the CD. Occasionally, you'll hear some melody notes even on the accompaniment tracks to reinforce the tune when the Boomwhacker® melody part may be difficult for some players. Of course, students may also play along with the full performance tracks. When needed, clicks sound at the start of each track to set the tempo and allow students to prepare to play. These tracks are indicated at the beginning of each music score.

Occasionally, tremolos or rolls or even repeated pitches appear because the tubes make a staccato rather than a sustaining sound. Practice the tremolos (some teachers may prefer to call them "rolls") by having students hold an empty hand close to the floor, thigh, or other playing surface and quickly bounce the tube back and forth between the surface and the hand (fingers or palm). Another way is to sit on the floor with feet about five inches apart and bounce the tube back and forth between the shoe soles. Tennis shoes work great! If the student is standing with feet shoulder-width apart, the tubes can be bounced between knees. Experiment!

Octavator™ caps are available for Boomwhacker® tubes, and they are super! These caps easily attach to either end of the tube and lower the tube's pitch by an octave, creating a very resonant sound. When using the caps, students can hold the tube perpendicular to the floor and gently bounce the capped end of the tube on the floor. The sound is best on a lightly carpeted surface; strips of felt can be placed on a hard surface. Use the caps or the bass tubes whenever you see *8vb* below the notes in arrangements within this book. (In the "Required Tubes" section, these are listed as "Low" pitches.) Many arrangements suggest *8vb* throughout the accompaniment part so that it sounds in the range of most left-hand piano parts.

To perform all ten songs in this book, it will require the use of at least set of the eight C Major Diatonic Scale tubes and one set of the Bass Diatonic (seven) tubes. Another option (preferred by the editor) is to use two C Major Diatonic sets and place Octavator ™ caps on one set. Additional sets provide more teaching flexibility, allowing students to hold a tube in each hand or to have several students play tubes of the same pitch. Of the ten classic works in this book, four ("Spinning Song," "The Merry Widow," "Can-Can," and "William Tell Overture") use chromatic tubes, which are optional but recommended to fill out the arrangement. This is indicated in the "Tubes Required" section for each title.

The arrangements in this book will provide you with opportunities to incorporate other Orff instruments and elements of movement into the Boomwhacker® ensemble. Three of the arrangements include Soprano Descant Recorder parts ("Rondeau Theme," "William Tell Overture," and "The Trout"). Several will easily transfer to barred instruments ("Turkish March," "Spinning Song," "Rondeau Theme," "Hopak," "Can-Can," and 'William Tell Overture"). Several titles ("Slavonic Dance," "Spinning Song," "Rondeau Theme," "Hopak," and "Can-Can") are obvious choices for addition of choreographed movement to enhance the performance. Finally, chord symbols have been added in this book in case you would like to accompany your students on piano or guitar or reference the harmonic changes for teaching purposes.

These arrangements were written for upper elementary and middle school general music classes. The scores provide both melody and accompaniment parts, although you may prefer to teach only one part or one section of the piece. Basic unpitched percussion is sometimes included to enhance the arrangement and provide varied playing opportunities for your students. All parts can be heard on the full performance CD tracks. Parts in the visuals and on the score are shown in treble clef or tenor clef, which is used to indicate pitches below middle C to be played with the bass tubes or tubes with Octavator™ caps. See the teaching suggestions for each song for more ideas on instrument use.

Finally, have fun! These are familiar songs that students will be eager to play—and now they can play them on the fun Boomwhacker® musical tubes.

—the Editor

CONTENTS

Editor's Note

This songbook is one of a series of materials for Boomwhackers® Musical Tubes being jointly developed by Warner Bros. Publications and Whacky Music, Inc., which manufactures Boomwhackers®. Whacky Music recognizes the important value these materials add to its unique musical tubes and is proud to have the opportunity to cooperate with Warner Bros. Publications in their development.

The color-coded, plastic Boomwhackers® tubes were invented by Craig Ramsell, president of Whacky Music, after being inspired by a cardboard gift-wrap tube that he had cut in two in preparation for recycling. As of this writing in 2003, more than one million Boomwhackers® have been shipped into the world. Because they are fun, easy to play, and inexpensive, a large number of them are being used in thousands of schools around the world for music education. They have received numerous awards, including a Parents' Choice Gold Award, Dr. Toy's Best 100 Children's Products, and an Oppenheim Toy Portfolio Gold Seal.

Turkish March

(from *The Ruins of Athens,* Op. 113)
by Ludwig van Beethoven

Tubes required:

(For the "Low" tubes, use bass tubes or tubes with Octavator™ caps.)

Pattern 1: F C
  Assign both tubes to one student.
Pattern 2: D A
  Assign both tubes to one student.

Pattern 3: C G
  Assign both tubes to one student.

Tremolo 1: Low E
  Assign one tube to each of two students.
Tremolo 2: Low A
  Assign one or two tubes to one student.
Tremolo 3: Low D Low B
  Assign one or two tubes to one student.

Unpitched percussion: Wood blocks, tambourine

Teaching suggestions:

- Use the accompaniment visual to show the different parts of the song. Photocopy as a transparency, or enlarge for all students to see. Distribute the tubes as suggested above. Group the students by the accompaniment part (patterns or tremolos) they play, next to each other in order of their entries.
- Teach the rhythm of Patterns 1 and 2. These patterns share the same two single-measure rhythms, although Pattern 2 has the rhythm in opposite order of Pattern 1. First practice by patting legs with hands. Pattern 1: Pitch F on left leg, Pitch C on right leg; Pattern 2: Pitch D on left leg, Pitch A on right leg.

Next, transfer to correct pitches on Boomwhackers® for Patterns 1 and 2.
- Explain to the students that *P1A* means they play only the first measure of Pattern 1, and *P1B* means they play only the second measure of Pattern 1. Similarly, *P3B* means the second measure of Pattern 3 is played.
- Use the accompaniment visual to play the patterns in order with the CD accompaniment.

 Note: The rhythm of Patterns 1 and 2 stays constant. However, a few times in the score, only one measure of the pattern is played as noted by the pattern labels, P1A, P1B, and P3B.
- Teach the three tremolo patterns and use the form visual to play in order.
- Combine patterns and tremolos with CD accompaniment.
- Using the visual, teach the coda. Assign to pitches C and F.
- Teach unpitched percussion (Wood blocks and tambourine) using the visual.

 Note: The tambourine has two different rhythms. It changes to steady eighth notes when the tremolos enter.
- Play the entire accompaniment with CD accompaniment.

Extension possibilities:

- Create a new rhythm for Patterns 1 and 2. For example:

- Transfer to barred Orff instruments as follows:
  - Patterns 1 and 2: Bass xylophone
  - Tremolos: Glockenspiels or alto xylophones

Visual

Turkish March
(from *The Ruins of Athens*, Op. 113)

LUDWIG VAN BEETHOVEN
Arranged by CHRIS JUDAH-LAUDER

ACCOMPANIMENT

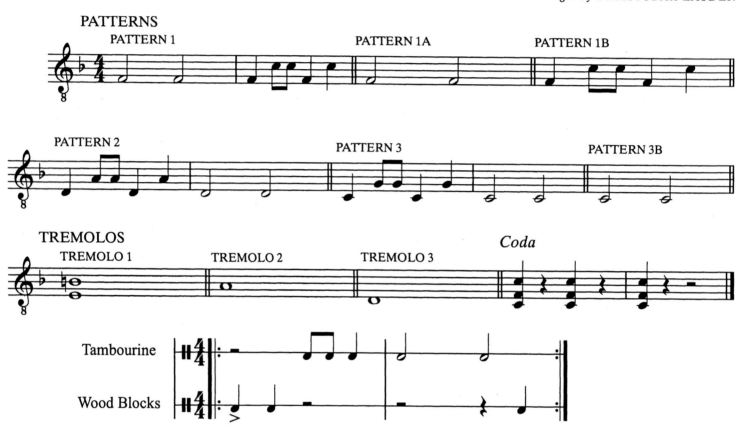

Visual

Turkish March
(from *The Ruins of Athens*, Op. 113)

FORM

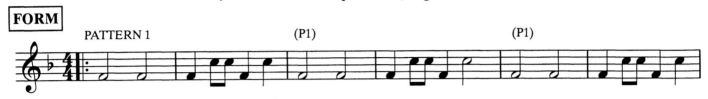

© 2004 BELWIN-MILLS PUBLISHING CORP.
All Rights Administered by WARNER BROS. PUBLICATIONS U.S. INC.
All Rights Reserved

Turkish March
(from *The Ruins of Athens*, Op. 113)

LUDWIG VAN BEETHOVEN
Arranged by CHRIS JUDAH-LAUDER

When using CD, wait for 4 clicks.

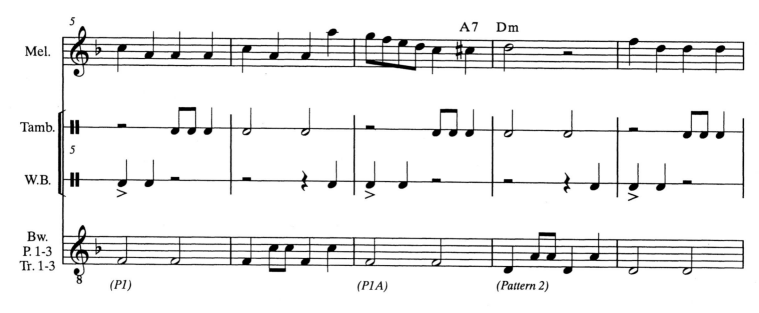

Hungarian Dance No. 5
by Johannes Brahms

Tubes required:

(For the "Low" tubes, use bass tubes or tubes with Octavator™ caps.)

Pattern 1: Low E   Low A
   Assign both tubes to one student.
   Pattern 1 player also plays the last measure of the song (coda).

Pattern 2: Low B
   Assign one or two tubes to one student.

Pattern 3: Low A
   Assign one or two tubes to one student.

Pattern 4: Low F   Low E   Low D   Low C
   Divide between four students, one tube each.

Teaching suggestions:

• Seat the students in groups based on the pattern they are playing.
• Teach all patterns by rote or use the accompaniment visual.
• Teach the sequence patterns. Provide a visual to indicate the form.

Sequence of Patterns:

1	1	2	3
3	3	2	3
1	1	2	1
	4	Coda	

• Combine patterns with CD accompaniment.

Extension possibilities:

• Add simple unpitched percussion.
• Encourage the students to create their own movement when their part is played.

Visual

Hungarian Dance No. 5

JOHANNES BRAHMS
Arranged by CHRIS JUDAH-LAUDER

ACCOMPANIMENT

PATTERNS

PATTERN 1

PATTERN 2

PATTERN 3

PATTERN 4   *Coda*

Warner Bros. Publications grants permission to the purchaser/owner of
this publication to photocopy only the visual pages for educational use only.

Hungarian Dance No. 5

When using CD, wait for 4 clicks.

JOHANNES BRAHMS
Arranged by CHRIS JUDAH-LAUDER

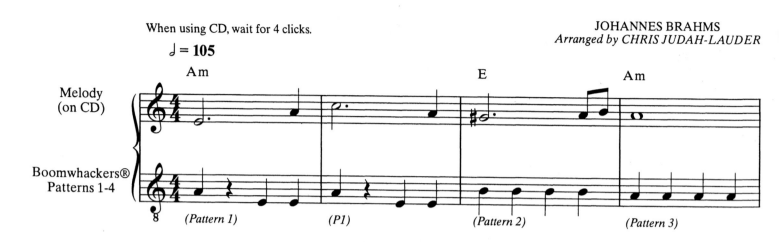

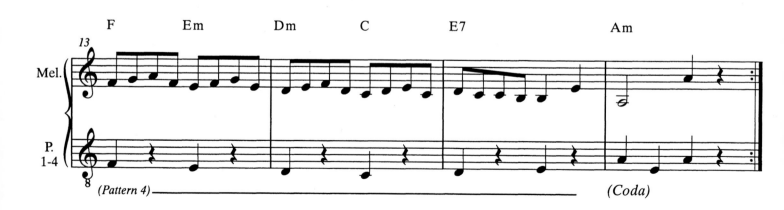

(Pattern 4) ————————————————— (Coda)

Slavonic Dance

(Op. 46, No. 7)

by Antonín Dvořák

Tubes required:

(For the "Low" tubes, use bass tubes or tubes with Octavator™ caps.)

Pattern 1:   A   High C
Assign both tubes to one student.
Pattern 2:   G   B
Assign both tubes to one student.
Pattern 3:   F   A
Assign both tubes to one student.
Pattern 4:   E   G
Assign both tubes to one student.
Pattern 5:   E
Assign tube to one student, or it can be played by Pattern 4 player.
Harmony: Low C   Low D
   Assign both tubes to one student.

Teaching suggestions:

- Using the accompaniment visual, teach Patterns 1–4.
- Group the students by pattern from left to right beginning with Pattern 1.
- Use the accompaniment visual to teach the form. Practice with and without the CD accompaniment.
- Use the accompaniment visual to teach the harmony. (This part is optional.)
  Combine harmony with Patterns 1–5.
- Play the entire accompaniment with CD accompaniment.

Extension possibilities:

- Transfer the melody to any C instrument. It may be necessary to change the melody slightly at the first and second endings:

- Add guitar or autoharp accompaniment. (See chord symbols.)
- Add movement.
- Arrange the students in lines facing the audience.

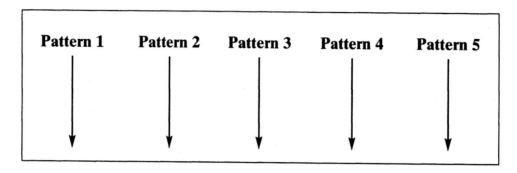

- When it is their turn to play, students play tubes and "cast off"* to the right in their own pattern line.
- Arrange the students playing the harmony part to stand at the sides of the Pattern 1 and Pattern 5 students.

*A cast-off is a movement commonly found in dance and musical theatre when the performers are arranged in a line facing the audience. The performer at the front of the line will peel off to the right or left and make their way to the back of the line. The next performer in line assumes the position at the front of the line and will be the next to cast off at the appropriate time.

Slavonic Dance
(Op. 46, No. 7)

When using CD, wait for 4 clicks.

ANTONÍN DVOŘÁK
Arranged by CHRIS JUDAH-LAUDER

Visual

Slavonic Dance
(Op. 46, No. 7)

ANTONÍN DVOŘÁK
Arranged by CHRIS JUDAH-LAUDER

ACCOMPANIMENT

PATTERNS

(PATTERN 1)   (PATTERN 2)

(PATTERN 3)   (PATTERN 4)   (PATTERN 5)

Form

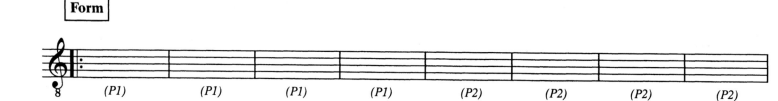

(P1)   (P1)   (P1)   (P1)   (P2)   (P2)   (P2)   (P2)

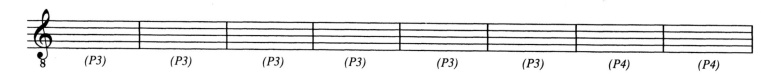

(P3)   (P3)   (P3)   (P3)   (P3)   (P3)   (P4)   (P4)

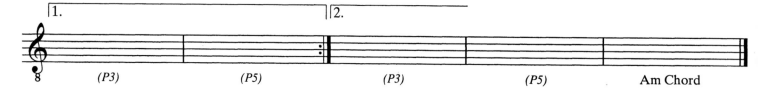

1.   2.

(P3)   (P5)   (P3)   (P5)   Am Chord

Harmony

Spinning Song
by Albert Ellmenreich

Tubes required:

(For the "Low" tubes, use bass tubes or tubes with Octavator™ caps.)

Pattern 1: Low   F   C
  Assign both tubes to one student.

Pattern 2: Low   C
  Assign one or two tubes to one student.
  If possible, have several students play this part.

Motive 1: G   A
  Assign both tubes to one student.

Motive 2: E   F
  Assign both tubes to one student.

Motive 3: G   A♭   A   B♭ (This motive is optional.)
  Divide between four students, one tube each.
  If necessary, substitute an F for the A♭.

Motive 4: B   High C
  Assign both tubes to one student.

Unpitched percussion: Shaker

Teaching suggestions:

- Use the accompaniment visual to teach the patterns, motives, and form.
- Group students with like patterns/motives.
- Teach Patterns 1 and 2. When teaching Pattern 2, point out the rhythmic change in measure 18.
  (Pattern 2 ends on a quarter note.) Combine with the CD accompaniment.
- Add shaker. Note the change of rhythm in the last measure.
- Teach Motives 1–4. Combine with Patterns 1 and 2 and CD accompaniment.
- Play the entire orchestration.

Extension possibilities:

- Add movement as follows.
  - Assign specific positions.
  - Motive players stand behind pattern players.
      Pattern players sit on the floor in front of motive players and sit next to like patterns.
  - Motive 1 and Motive 2 players spin in place on rests. Nod head from side to side and play
    two assigned notes in pattern.
  - Motive 3 and Motive 4 players are standing in order (see score).
      When playing Motive 3 the first time, bend down on one knee and hit tube on knee.
      When playing Motive 3 the second time, stand up and hit tube against the other hand.
      Note: Motive 4 can also play on the last measure of the song.
  - Pattern players (sitting on floor in front of motive players) may hit tube against floor or legs.
- Transfer accompaniment to barred Orff instruments as follows:
  - Patterns 1–4: Bass and alto xylophone
  - Motives 1–4: Glockenspiels (in Motive 3, change A♭ to F)

Visual

Spinning Song

ALBERT ELLMENREICH
Arranged by CHRIS JUDAH-LAUDER

ACCOMPANIMENT

MOTIVES

Shaker

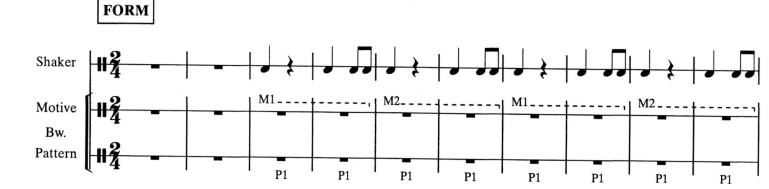

FORM

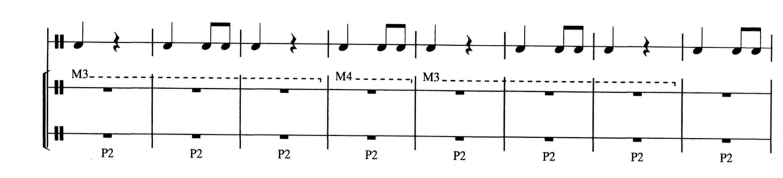

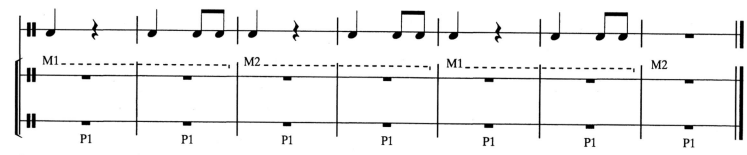

Spinning Song

ALBERT ELLMENREICH
Arranged by CHRIS JUDAH-LAUDER

When using CD, wait for 4 clicks.

Spinning Song - 2 - 1

20

Spinning Song - 2 - 2

Theme
(from *The Merry Widow*)

by Franz Lehár

Tubes required:

F Maj: F   A   C
Divide among three students, one tube each.

C Maj: C   E   G
Divide among three students, one tube each.

C Maj: G   B
Divide among two students, one tube each.

D min: D   F   A
Divide among three students, one tube each.

E Maj: E   G♯ (opt.)   B
Divide among three students, one tube each.

Teaching suggestions:

- Depending on how many tubes you have, evenly divide the class into four chords (F Maj, C Maj, G Maj, D min, and E Maj). Group students according to their assigned chord.
- To simplify, have each student participate in only one chord, even if his or her pitch is common to more than one. As a test to be sure each student knows what chord is his or hers, have each group stand when you call out the name of their chord.
- If you have a limited number of students, strive to have at least two different pitches in each chord.
- Using the visual, play the recording and ask students to listen and follow along with the music. (The melody line is provided to assist for easy entrances of tubes.)
- Practice each chord separately using a tremolo effect. Point out whether it is to be held three or six counts. Define *tie*: A tie is a curved line joining two notes of like pitch that are to be sounded as one note equal to their united time value. (*Tremolo* is explained in the General Teaching Suggestions on page 2.)
- Next, practice the chords in sequence (without the CD) using the visual accompaniment as a guide for order (measures 5–8, 13–16, 23–24, and 29–32).
- Play the entire song with the recording. Have students sway from right to left when they are not playing.

Extension possibilities:

- Instead of using a tremolo on the chords, try using the rhythms outlined in the following example, which corresponds to measures 5–7. Use the same rhythm on other measures when chords enter.

- Add guitar or autoharp accompaniment.

Visual

Theme
(from *The Merry Widow*)

FRANZ LEHÁR
Arranged by CHRIS JUDAH-LAUDER

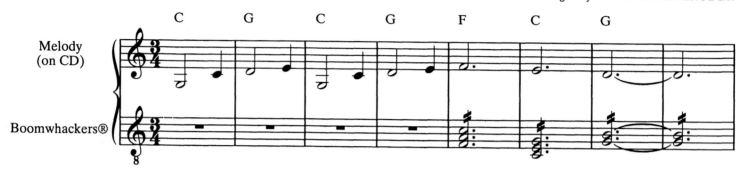

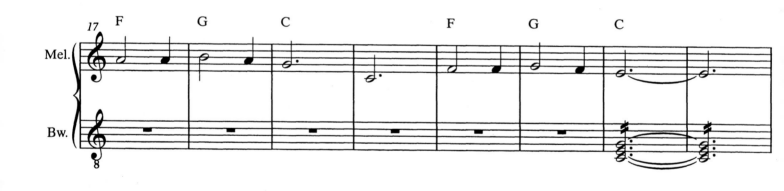

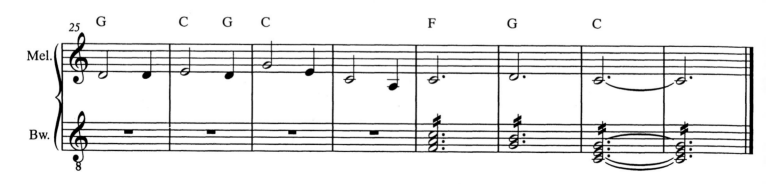

© 2004 BELWIN-MILLS PUBLISHING CORP.
All Rights Administered by WARNER BROS. PUBLICATIONS U.S. INC.
All Rights Reserved

Theme
(from *The Merry Widow*)

When using CD, wait for 3 clicks.

FRANZ LEHÁR
Arranged by CHRIS JUDAH-LAUDER

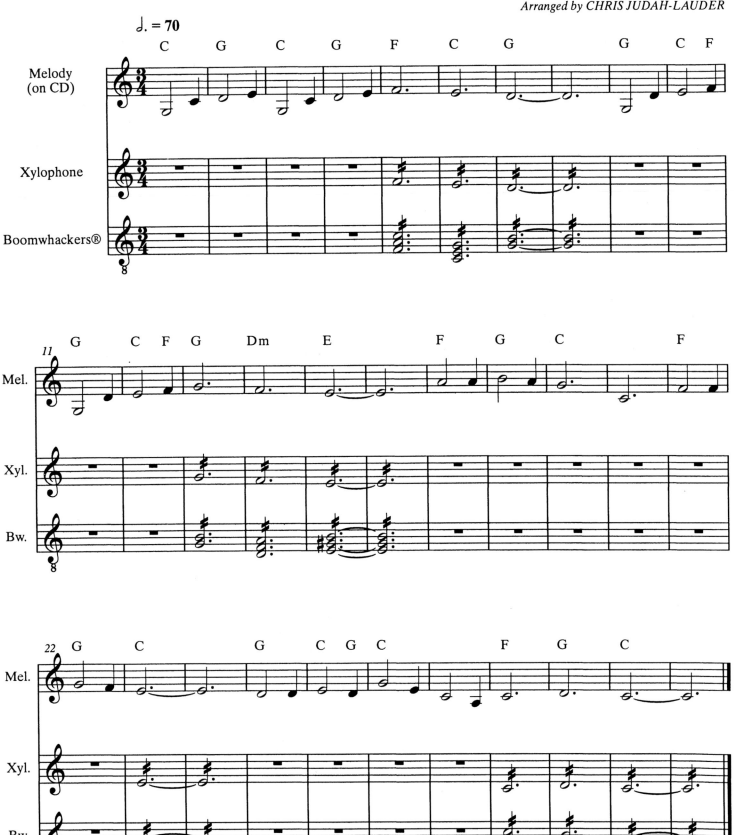

Rondeau Theme
(from Symphonic Suite No. 1)
by Jean-Joseph Mouret

Tubes required:

(For the "Low" tubes, use bass tubes or tubes with Octavator™ caps.)

Pattern 1: Low or High C
Divide between two students, each having two like tubes.

Pattern 2: Low G
Assign one tube to one or several students.

Other instruments: Wood blocks, cabasa (or shaker), hand drum, soprano recorder (optional)

Teaching suggestions:

- This is a very easy piece to teach by rote. No visual is necessary unless you want the students to follow the melody line.
- The rhythm is identical for both patterns; only the pitch is different. Have the students practice clapping the rhythm while you speak the text:

Down a la - zy road.

- Listen to the CD and clap the above rhythm as the song is played.
- Now have the students play the rhythm on Boomwhackers®, both C and G. The sequence of patterns in the song consists of two measures of Pattern 1 followed by two measures of Pattern 2 (see score).
  Note: Notice the change in the sequence in the last two measures of the song (one measure of Pattern 2 followed by one measure of Pattern 1).
- Using a visual, teach the following unpitched percussion:

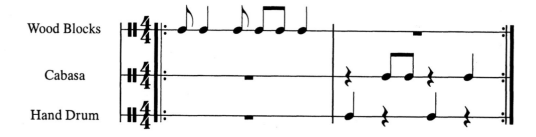

- Combine Boomwhackers® and unpitched percussion with the CD accompaniment. Assist by cueing each group as its pattern comes up.
- Finally, as an option, teach the soprano recorder part. Use the Soprano Recorder Visual to assist you.

Extension possibilities:

- Add movement as follows:
    - Arrange students in two lines facing each other, one line with C tubes and the other with G tubes.
    - Instruct students to move forward when playing and move backward when not playing. Once again, remind students about the change on the last two measures.
    - Have the unpitched percussion players (and soprano recorder players) move in a circle around the two lines in the following order: wood blocks, hand drum, cabasa, recorder. Feel free to double up on these parts.
- Add guitar accompaniment.

Visual:
Soprano Recorder

Rondeau Theme
(from Symphonic Suite No. 1)

JEAN-JOSEPH MOURET
Arranged by CHRIS JUDAH-LAUDER

♩ = 120

© 2004 BELWIN-MILLS PUBLISHING CORP.
All Rights Administered by WARNER BROS. PUBLICATIONS U.S. INC.
All Rights Reserved

Rondeau Theme
(from Symphonic Suite No. 1)

When using CD, wait for 3 clicks.

JEAN-JOSEPH MOURET
Arranged by CHRIS JUDAH-LAUDER

Hopak
by Modest Mussorgsky

Tubes required:

(This piece can be played with or without Octavator™ caps.)

C chord: Low C   E   G   High C
Divide among four students, one tube each.
The *P1* in the last measure indicates a slight rhythm change.

G7 chord: G   B   D   F
Divide among four students, one tube each.

Other instruments: Xylophone (optional)

Teaching suggestions:

- Group the students according to their assigned chord.
      Note: There will be G tubes in both groups, but the students should play only on their assigned chord.
- Listen to the CD accompaniment. As the song plays, point to the group that will play at each entrance point. Take time to clarify measures 5, 6, and 8 where only C's play.
- Teach Boomwhacker® parts by rote.
- Combine with the CD accompaniment. Assist by cueing each group.
- Add movement as follows:
  - Arrange the students in concentric circles. Students playing the G7 chord should form the inner circle and face clockwise. Students playing the C chord should form the outer circle and face counterclockwise.
    - Measures 1–4:
      - The inner circle (G7 chord) marches clockwise. The tube is held in the right hand, resting on the right shoulder.
      - The outer circle (C chord) marches counterclockwise and plays, hitting the tube against the other hand.
    - Measures 5–6:
      - Both circles abruptly stop in place (see score).
      - Students holding Low or High C play, hitting the tube against the other hand above their heads.
    - Measures 7–8:
      - Students holding Low or High C once again play by hitting the tube against the other hand above their heads.
      - During these two measures, the inner circle switches places with the outer circle (see score). Instruct the students to travel to the closest point possible in their new circle. The students should be in the same order in the circle as before. Remind the C tube players to keep playing their part as they travel.
    - Measures 9–16:
      - The inner circle (C chord) marches counterclockwise, with the tube held in the right hand, resting on the right shoulder. The outer circle (G7 chord) marches clockwise and plays, hitting the tube against the other hand.

- Measures 17–20:
  - Switch direction. The inner circle (C chord) now marches clockwise and plays, hitting the tube against the other hand.
  - The outer circle (G7 chord) marches counterclockwise, with the tube held in the right hand, resting on the right shoulder.
- Measures 21–22:
  - The students now form one large circle. As before, the movement should be quick and efficient, and the students playing the C chord should continue to play as they travel.
  - In the new circle, the students should face inward and play as notated in the score. Students in the C chord should play, hitting the tube against their other hand. Students holding the G7 chord should hold the tube in their right hand and rest it on their right shoulder.
- Measures 23–24 (Coda):
  - The students are still in one large circle, facing inward. On the first beat of the last measure (24) students playing the C chord play the final chord by softly hitting the elbow of the other arm while looking up. The students playing the G7 chord drop to their knees, hold the tube between both hands parallel to the floor, and look down.

Extension possibilities:

- Teach the optional xylophone part by rote and combine it with the other parts.

Hopak

When using CD, wait for 4 clicks.

MODEST MUSSORGSKY
Arranged by CHRIS JUDAH-LAUDER

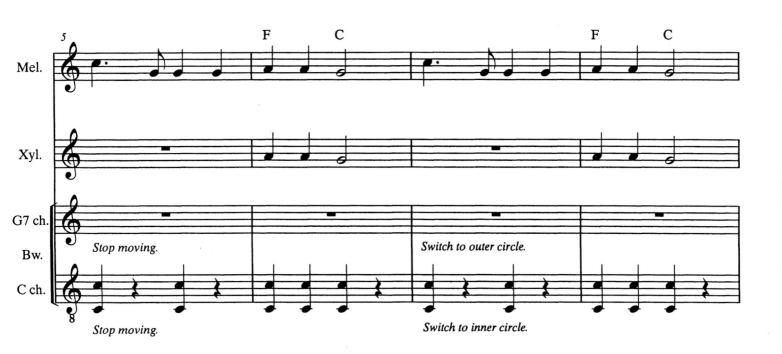

Hopak - 2 - 1

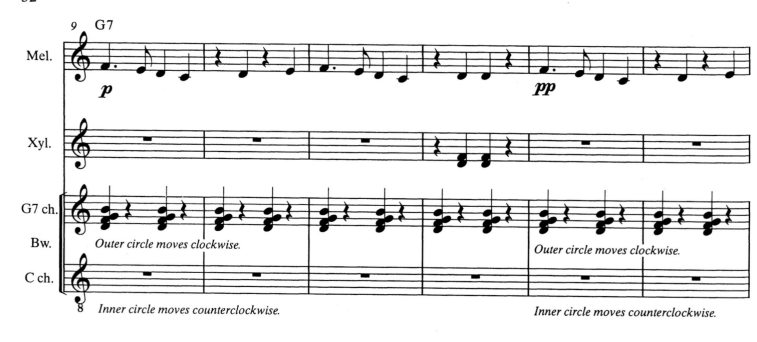

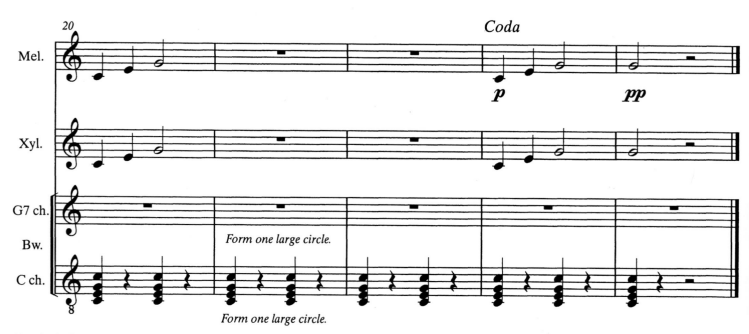

Can-Can
(from *Orphée aux enfers*)
by Jacques Offenbach

Tubes required:

(For the "Low" tubes, use bass tubes or tubes with Octavator™ caps.)

Pattern 1: Low C   Low G
   Assign both tubes to one student.

Pattern 2: (C chord)   Low C   Low E   Low G   High C
   Assign one tube to each of four students.

Pattern 3: (B♭ chord)   Low D   Low F   Low B♭
   Assign one tube to each of three players; if necessary, omit the B♭.

Pattern 4: Low E   Low F
   Assign both tubes to one student.

Pattern 5: Low G
   Assign tube(s) to one or two students, or have the G tube player from Pattern 2 also play Pattern 5.

Interlude: F
   Assign tube(s) to one or two students.

Teaching suggestions:

- Teach all parts by rote or use the accompaniment visual.
- Teach the sequence of patterns. Provide a visual to indicate the form (see below). The numbers refer to the pattern, and the whole rests indicate four counts where no Boomwhackers® are played.

1	1		
2	3	4	5
2	3	4	4
𝄻	4	𝄻	4
Interlude			

- Add movement as follows:
  - Arrange the students into three rows, as follows:
    Pattern 1: Stand in back row.
    Patterns 2–5: Kneel on one knee in the middle row, in front of the Pattern 1 players.
    Interlude: Sit in the front row.

- Assign movement to each pattern (also outlined in the accompaniment visual) as follows:
  - Pattern 1:
  During the first two measures of Pattern 1, the C's and G's are played by lifting one leg and hitting the Boomwhacker® on the leg, alternating legs for every note. During the second two measures of Pattern 1, the G's are played by hitting the Boomwhacker® against the other wrist, high over the head while panning from left to right.
  - Patterns 2–5:
  When Patterns 2–5 are not playing, they are kneeling on one knee in the middle row. After each pattern plays, the students jump into the air (on beat 1) as they hit the Boomwhacker® against their other hand. They return to the kneeling position when another pattern starts to play.
  - Measures 19 and 21 (rests):
  All players stand and wave their Boomwhackers® over their heads as they turn in a circle in place. (Students who are not already standing should jump to their feet on beat 4 of measure 18.) The students should make one complete turn in each measure so they are all facing forward on beat 1 of measures 20 and 22.
  - Measures 20 and 22:
  Pattern 4 is played while other players stand still, facing forward.
  - Interlude:
  Back row (Pattern 1): March in place.
  Middle row (Patterns 2–5): Sway back and forth, from right to left.
  Front row (Interlude): Play by hitting Boomwhackers® on the floor while sitting. (Students in the front row should sit down on beat 4 of measure 22.) During the interlude, Patterns 2–5 should return to the kneeling position for the repeat.

Extension possibilities:

- See the visual accompaniment for the advanced rhythm for Pattern 1.
- Transfer to barred Orff instruments as follows:
  - Pattern 1: Bass xylophone
  - Pattern 2: Bass metallophone
  - Pattern 3: Alto xylophones/metallophones
  - Pattern 4: Soprano xylophones/metallophones
  - Pattern 5: Glockenspiels
  - Interlude: All barred instruments play on pitch F.
- Combine all extension possibilities with the Boomwhacker® arrangement.

Visual

Can-Can
(from *Orphée aux enfers*)

JACQUES OFFENBACH
Arranged by CHRIS JUDAH-LAUDER

ACCOMPANIMENT

PATTERNS

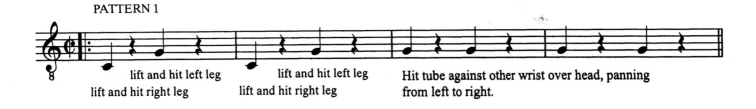

PATTERN 1

lift and hit left leg

lift and hit right leg

lift and hit left leg

lift and hit right leg

Hit tube against other wrist over head, panning
from left to right.

Patterns 2-5: Jump up in the air on beat 1 and hit Boomwhacker® against other hand.

PATTERN 2   PATTERN 3   PATTERN 4   PATTERN 5

INTERLUDE

PATTERN 1
(advanced)

Can-Can
(from *Orphée aux enfers*)

When using CD, wait for 4 clicks.

JACQUES OFFENBACH
Arranged by CHRIS JUDAH-LAUDER

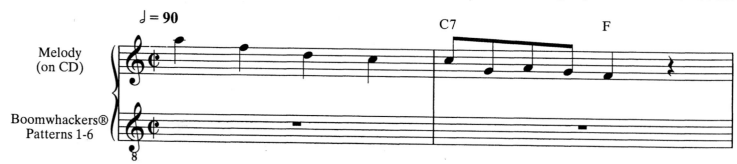

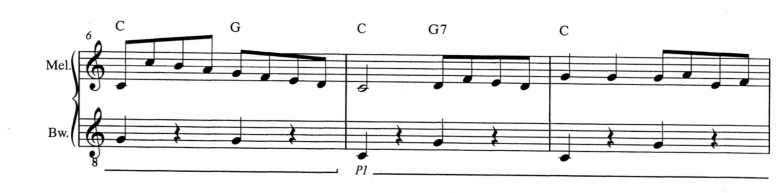

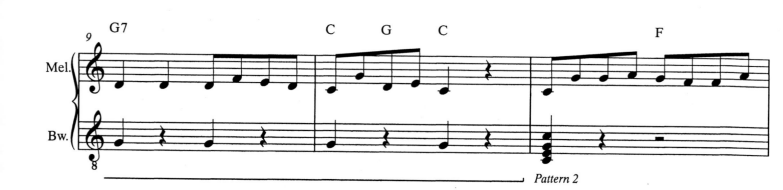

William Tell Overture
(Theme)
by Gioacchino Rossini

Tubes required:

(For the "Low" tubes, use bass tubes or tubes with Octavator™ caps.)

Pattern 1: Low G   Low B Low   Low D
   Assign G and B to one player, and one or two D's to one player.

Pattern 2: Low D
   Assign one or two tubes to one player.

Pattern 3: Low G
   Assign one or two tubes to one player.

Pattern 4: Low D   F♯ (opt.)
   Assign one or two tube(s) to one player for each pitch.

Other instruments: Xylophone and/or soprano recorder

Teaching suggestions:

• Group the students based on the pattern they are playing.
• Teach Patterns 1–3 by rote. Use a visual to teach the sequence of patterns (see below):

1	**2**
1	**3**
Interlude	

• Combine Patterns 1–3 with the CD accompaniment.
• Teach Pattern 4 by rote. See visual.
• Teach the interlude by rote. See Visual.

• Teach the optional xylophone/soprano recorder part by rote, or use the visual accompaniment. If you have advanced players, the melody could also be played on any instrument.
• Play the entire Boomwhacker® accompaniment with the CD accompaniment.

Extension possibilities:

• Add barred Orff instruments.
• Transfer Patterns 1–3 to bass xylophone.
    Change Pattern 1 to pitches G, rest, G, G.
    Patterns 2 and 3 remain the same.
• Transfer Pattern 4 to alto or soprano xylophone.
• Transfer xylophone/soprano recorder to glockenspiel.

William Tell Overture
(Theme)

GIOACCHINO ROSSINI
Arranged by CHRIS JUDAH-LAUDER

Visual

ACCOMPANIMENT

PATTERNS

PATTERN 1

PATTERN 2

PATTERN 3

PATTERN 4

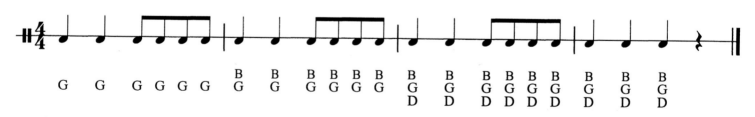

Interlude

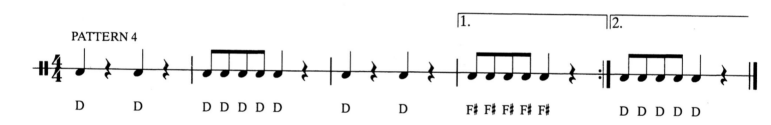

© 2004 BELWIN-MILLS PUBLISHING CORP.
All Rights Administered by WARNER BROS. PUBLICATIONS U.S. INC.
All Rights Reserved

William Tell Overture
(Theme)

Visual:
Soprano Recorder/Xylophone

GIOACCHINO ROSSINI
Arranged by CHRIS JUDAH-LAUDER

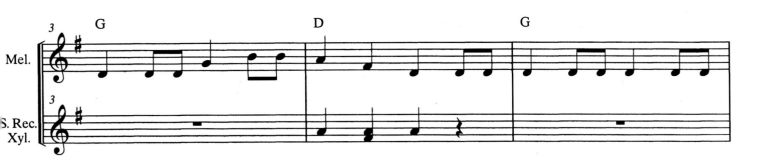

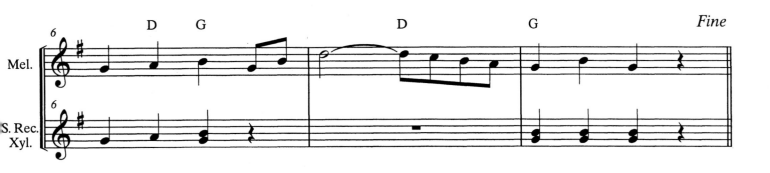

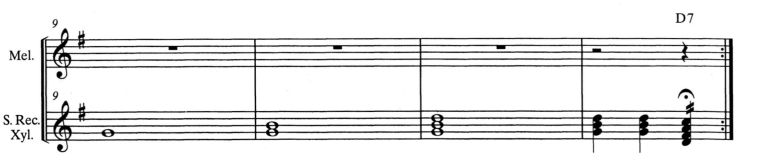

© 2004 BELWIN-MILLS PUBLISHING CORP.
All Rights Administered by WARNER BROS. PUBLICATIONS U.S. INC.
All Rights Reserved

William Tell Overture
(Theme)

When using CD, wait for 3 clicks.

GIOACCHINO ROSSINI
Arranged by CHRIS JUDAH-LAUDER

Melody (onCD)

Xylophone Soprano Rec.

Boomwhacker® Pattern 4

Boomwhacker® Patterns 1-3

(Pattern 1)

(Pattern 2)

5

Mel.

Xyl. S. Rec.

Bw. P. 4

Bw. P. 1-3

Fine

(P1)

(Pattern 3)

Interlude

9

Mel.

Xyl. S. Rec.

Bw. P. 4

Bw. P. 1-3

D7

Theme From "The Trout" Quintet (1819)

by Franz Schubert

Tubes required:

(For the "Low" tubes, use bass tubes or tubes with Octavator™ caps.)

Pattern 1: Low C
   Assign one or two tubes to one player.

Pattern 2: Low D
   Assign one or two tubes to one player.

Pattern 3: Low G
   Assign one or two tubes to one player.

Unpitched percussion: Güiro (Optional)

Optional descant: Soprano recorder

Teaching suggestions:

- Using the visual accompaniment, teach Patterns 1–3. Use the form visual to keep the parts in order. Note that Patterns 2 and 3 have common entrances at measures 3, 7, and 15.
- Teach the interlude by rote.
- Teach the güiro part. Note the rhythm change in the fourth and eighth measures.
- Play the entire accompaniment with the CD accompaniment.

Extension possibilities:

- Add a descant using the Soprano Recorder Visual.

Visual

Theme From "The Trout" Quintet (1819)

FRANZ SCHUBERT
Arranged by CHRIS JUDAH-LAUDER

ACCOMPANIMENT

FORM

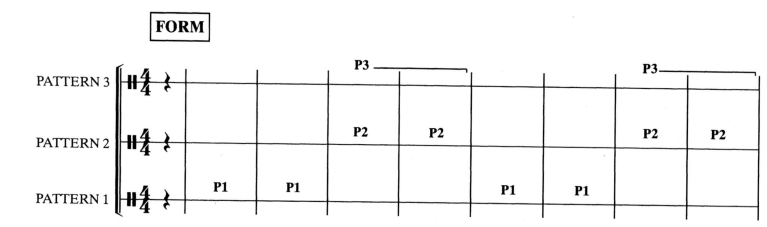

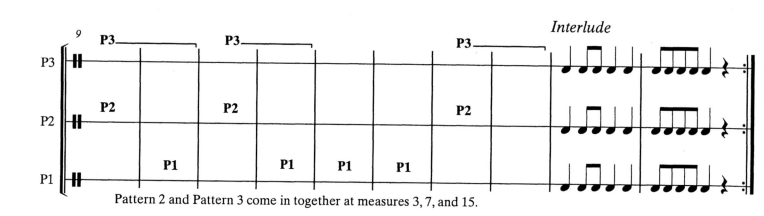

Pattern 2 and Pattern 3 come in together at measures 3, 7, and 15.

GÜIRO

Theme From "The Trout" Quintet (1819)

FRANZ SCHUBERT
Arranged by CHRIS JUDAH-LAUDER

Visual:
Soprano Recorder & Melody

Fine

Interlude

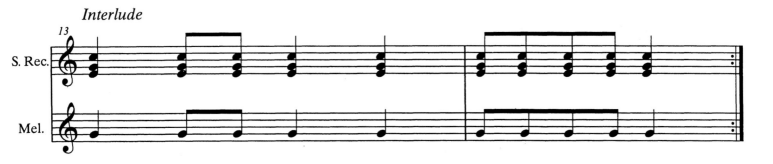

Theme From "The Trout" Quintet (1819)

When using CD, wait for 3 clicks.

FRANZ SCHUBERT
Arranged by CHRIS JUDAH-LAUDER

The Trout - 2 - 1

About the Author

CHRIS JUDAH-LAUDER

Chris teaches music at Good Shepherd Episcopal School in Dallas, Tex where she received the Teacher of the Year Award in 2001. She has served the regional representative for the national board of the American Or Schulwerk Association and was elected as local conference co-chair the 1995 National Orff-Schulwerk Conference held in Dallas, Tex where her students performed for the opening session.

A nationally known clinician, she has taught Orff teacher traini courses and in-service staff developments and presents workshops 1 "children's music in church" throughout the United States.

As well as a clinician and presenter, she also directs three middle scho music ensemble groups that have been featured at many conferences including the opening session of the 1995 National Orff-Schulwe Conference, the 2000 International Percussive Arts Society Conference, tl Texas Music Educators' Association Conference, and Southwest Association Episcopal Schools, Chorister's Guild, and Independent Schools Association of the Southwe conferences—Children's Festivals in Houston, Dallas TV stations, and many other locations througho the Dallas metropolitan area.

In her spare time, Chris enjoys tending to her flowers, relaxing on the lake with her family, and feedir the birds.